Unexpected Change

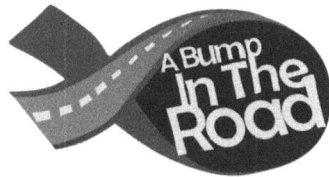

A Bump In The Road

Mary Jane Cronin MS, LMHC

Editor: Philip S Marks

Cover Design & Format: Ginger Marks
www.DocUmeantDesigns.com

Printed in The United States of America

ISBN: 978-0-9845016-3-2

Contents

Foreword

"Life is what happens to you while you're busy making other plans," said Allen Saunders in Reader's Digest magazine in January 1957, and how true that has proved to be in my life. While small changes can disrupt, especially if you're like me and thrive on routine; it's the major changes that rock your core.

When my four-year-old son breathed his last after eight months of cancer treatments, I knew my life would never be the same again and yet I didn't know just how gut-wrenching each day without him would be. There was no getting him back. He was gone from my life forever. I believed he was in Heaven, but questioned God. "Why did you let this happen? Daniel doesn't even know how to tie his shoes. He needs me. I need him."

Over time, my husband's mental and physical health declined. He drank heavily, and one summer afternoon, he left my three young children and me. I had a new challenge — single parenting. This was not how I had envisioned life for me or my kids.

Adapt. Adjust. One foot in front of the other. Pray. Write out the struggles and the emotions. Scream into the night air. I learned how all this is done.

Monumental changes like death, divorce, and debilitating health forces us to sink or swim. Hopefully we have friends and professionals to lean on for support as we navigate uncharted waters. Big changes make us evaluate new aspects of our daily lives and often we find ourselves changing our old values, relationships, work, finances, and even faith.

This gift of a book, *Unexpected Change,* by Mary Jane Cronin will wake you up to take a fresh look at the changes you are facing and how you are affected by them. Her lovingly-prepared advice that comes from her own personal heartache will show you how to grow from the sorrow, and live with perseverance and hope.

As long as there is breath, there is hope.

That's been my mantra. That has not changed.

Alice J. Wisler
Getting Out of Bed in the Morning: Reflections of Comfort in Heartache

Chapter One

Change Basics

There is a saying *"The only good change, is the change you find in your pocket."*

People often fear change, resist it, and even try to avoid it from happening. Change however, is a natural part of life and everyone faces it at one time or another. We begin to accept change when we have control of it. Change can be a positive thing. Our changing needs or interests in clothing, music, or dining is considered being "adventurous." Changing to a more efficient way to do a task at work is a being proactive.

There are several factors that determine our response to change. If the change suggests a gain, such as a new baby or a promotion at work, you may feel excited and look forward to the change.

On the other hand, you may worry about a change that involves a potential loss such as death or a divorce.

The amount of time you have to prepare for a change can influence your acceptance.

You may find it easier to make a gradual adjustment to something happening in a few weeks, but may find it stressful to face a sudden upheaval in your everyday life.

Accepting a sudden, unexpected change can be one of the most difficult challenges in life. You want to have control over the situation and make everything better, but no matter how hard you try, you just can't control everything. Learning to accept the reality that you do not have full control over what happens in your life, helps to make things easier to cope with.

> Focusing on what you can control, and trying to let go of what you can't is one of the best strategies for coping with change.

Everyone reacts differently to changes and unexpected events. Some people feel stress because of events that are happy ones, such as a wedding or the birth of a baby. Others enjoy the "rush" in planning the events as much as partaking in them.

Many people have trouble coping with divorce, a controversy at work, or a move to a new place to live.

The change does not need to be a large one for some people to be stressed. Smaller events such as an upcoming holiday, trouble with in-laws, or even a vacation can send some into panic mode. Even when you are looking forward to a change, adjusting to these new realities can be stressful. Having a support system in your life can help you adapt and begin coping with the difficulties.

Some people are just not good with change. They have intensely negative reactions when they first hear that they'll be facing a big change. Some people cry or become angry.

Others think, "It isn't fair, I'll never be able to handle this," or "I'm too old to learn a new way of doing things."

Depending on the nature of the change you face, you may want to turn to your family or friends, or possibly a support group whose members know what you're going through and want to help and support you.

Try to remember that a change — even if you didn't want it — can be beneficial and help you begin to change your own outlook.

SOME BENEFITS OF CHANGE

Education: Change that involves new experiences can bring greater knowledge, awareness, and the opportunity to develop a new skill.

Increase your flexibility: Changes in one area of your life can help you begin to make changes in other areas of your life as well.

Set priorities in your life: Being forced to make changes in your life often causes you to look at what is important to you. Realize what is valuable and what can be compromised.

Become mentally stronger: When you can accept change, you begin to look for positive components in that change. When new changes arise, you will be better equipped to handle them.

Build self-confidence: Learning to accept change creates growth. Staying in a comfortable situation is fine for a while, but most people need a challenge.

Change can bring new opportunities: Almost every new experience has both advantages and disadvantages. Focus on the aspects that you love, not what you dislike or fear.

Although change can bring new opportunities and be rewarding, it is often seen as stressful at first. Depending on the nature of your adjustment, the difficulties can last anywhere from a few days to several years.

> For some, change, like a loss, causes one to grieve for the life before the change. The responses can be both physically and mentally stressful.

The larger the change or impact of the change, the more stress you may face. Moving from one major stage of life to another such as adjusting to having a child, reaching midlife, becoming a step-parent or grandparent, becoming a caregiver, getting divorced, or beginning retirement are particularly difficult.

Change produces unique signals that people can learn to identify so they can respond to them sooner. The sooner they can begin to cope with their change and ultimate transition, the more likely they are to be effective in the change process.

Emotions — People need to be <u>aware</u> of their moods and feelings when they are experiencing changes. Some of these changes can produce feelings of anger, increased anxiety, moodiness, frustration, depression, and withdrawal. Their behaviors may also include unusual lashing out at others.

Mind — People need to be <u>aware</u> that they might have excessive negative thoughts. These thoughts may cause confusion, distraction, difficulty in concentrating or difficulty "turning their mind off" at night to sleep. At work, there may be a decrease in productivity or an increase in forgetfulness.

Body — People need to be <u>aware</u> of their body's physical symptoms such as an increase in headaches, colds, flu symptoms, digestion problems, minor aches and pains, major illnesses, feelings of exhaustions, and muscle aches and pains. These symptoms can be negative reactions to the change process.

SYMPTOMS OF STRESS FROM CHANGE

Physical symptoms can include headaches, heart problems, head, neck or backaches, stomach aches and digestive problems, and fatigue.

Emotional symptoms can include depression, mood swings, overeating or loss of appetite, anxiety, and insomnia.

Psychological symptoms can include poor concentration, forgetfulness, and feelings of hopelessness.

If you keep having these symptoms long after a change has occurred, you may want to talk to a doctor or counselor about ways to cope with stress.

TIPS FOR COPING WITH CHANGE

Someone to talk to: Talk to friends who've faced the same kind of change and ask what helped them in dealing with it. Be as specific as you can about your concerns. You might say to your neighbor, *"I have more responsibilities at work and it's become harder for me to make dinner every night. I know you began working full time recently, what has helped you? I'd like to hear your ideas on what you did about this."*

Support groups can help: If a change feels too big to handle alone, consider joining a group for people who are going through a similar experience. There are groups for step-parents, newcomers to a community, or caregivers for people with illnesses such as Alzheimer's or Parkinson's.

Journal: Write about your experiences in a journal. Start when you become faced with the unexpected change. Write about your feelings and the actions you are taking. Re-reading your journal later, once your emotions have subsided, may help you cope with changes more smoothly.

Research: The most stressful thing about change may be the uncertainty it brings. To ease your anxieties, learn as much as you can about what you'll be facing. Do research on the Internet or at the library.

Breath: You might find it helpful to take a yoga class or listen to relaxation tapes. These tapes are available online or at most bookstores and public libraries. Set aside a few minutes each day to visualize yourself being calm and happy.

Create a plan: Try to take small steps to "grow into" or adjust to the change. Plan positive goals.

If you know that you're already experiencing stress, if possible, try to postpone making big decisions that will bring about more change, and possibly, more stress. If you're facing a big change, take extra care to eat a healthy diet, exercise regularly, get enough sleep, and limit your alcohol and caffeine consumption.

In our changing society, many people find themselves fearing unexpected and often debilitating changes in their lives. Change reveals itself in various facets of a person's life.

Workplace: When facing a change at work, denying that change is or will be occurring only makes things more difficult. The more we understand that the change may happen, the less upset and surprised we will be when we encounter that change. Recognizing that change happens is desirable, but to recognize when change might be happening in your own specific situation is both healthy and pro-active.

Keep alert to subtle clues. Is your job in jeopardy? For example, are you being excluded from important meetings? Does your boss seem more distant towards you than in the past?

The work world is changing as people often find themselves experiencing a transition in their employment. Corporations have begun outsourcing jobs to other parts of the world and some jobs are being eliminated to save money. Retirement savings are diminishing or disappearing due to the changes in the economy and competition has increased for the remaining jobs.

Health: As society changes and people are finding themselves trying to keep up with the changes, they are experiencing more stress and anxiety. This leads to more physical illnesses, psychological problems, changes in eating habits, increased injuries, and sleeping issues.

Home & Family: Over the years there has been an increase in changes of family dynamics and the way people experience a sense of home and family. Home-life has changed as people marry, divorce, and have blended families. Single parents, by divorce, death, or personal choice may now need grandparents to take a more active role in raising their grandchildren.

Personal: Changes in people's personal and social lives may be some of the biggest changes people experience. Some of these changes include financial struggles due to overspending, major debt, and job loss. Personal cultural differences, changes in residence, and the struggle to keep up with changes in technology can all stressfully affect us.

Because of frequent changes in our daily lives, people face increasing levels of stress. Although change has always been a part of the lives of human beings, the present rate of changes is increasing.

It is the speed of this change that increases the stress in peoples' lives. Change is not going to stop, and therefore, people must develop new skills to manage stress more carefully. Coping with change is a critical life skill that can be the difference between living a life of success or one of disappointment.

Moving through a change can be difficult. There will be good days of acceptance and bad days of anger. No matter what the change may be, we all experience certain thoughts. These thoughts and emotions of change do not travel on a strictly predictable course and can reappear unexpectedly.

SHOCK—No matter what's happened or how much we may have prepared for impending changes, once a change has taken place, we often find ourselves in an initial state of shock. We are left wondering why it's happening to us.

People in this stage are often full of anxiety and attempt to deny the reality of current or future changes. We might say things like "It can't be true!"

ANGER—Initially, people feel anger toward those we believe are responsible for the change and blame them. In time, we may even begin to feel angry at ourselves and becomes self-critical.

The fear of change and the uncertainty of the future can have a negative effect on us. We may begin to question ourselves and wonder if we are competent and able to handle what's in store for us. Experiencing panic is common, as one begins to realize how the changes will impact them directly.

BARGAINING—When people feel threatened they often retreat to the safest belief system they can find. If we can point to external factors such as "unrealistic" demands or an unsteady economy, it might justify the cause of the change. This relieves us of all accountability and portrays us as a helpless victim in the matter—an easy and convenient escape.

Some people attempt to make a deal with their higher power or the people involved in the change process. If we attempt to compromise and that action fails, we usually give up and become depressed at our lack of control.

Questions can include "What can I do now?" or "Can you please give me another chance?" We try to identify our options and wish that things could be different.

DEPRESSION — Following a change, people may begin to feel sad or depressed and think there are limited or no options for them. We often become silent and withdrawn and begin to experience increasing weakness, discomfort, and personal deterioration. We can have feelings of self-doubt, insignificance, frustration, weariness, and a desire to be left alone. We may feel guilty and unworthy and feel as if nobody cares what happens to us.

ACCEPTANCE — People who reach the end of their struggle can now begin to accept that change happens to everyone. We see that changes can be overcome, and may even bring new opportunities. We begin to let go of our negative feelings. We notice that the pain begins to lessen and the struggle seems less difficult. We recognize that it is time to move on with our lives. We begin to accept our new "normal."

Our initial reaction to the unexpected is usually anything but constructive. We feel vulnerable and even threatened by the changes at hand, including those that we may have already anticipated. As we come to terms with the unknown, we tend to find ourselves in the midst of feelings of surprise, panic, and blame.

If you've experienced any of these emotions when faced with change, you are certainly not alone. But the reality is that none of these stages will help us cope with what's in front of us.

Why? Because none of them get to the core of the real problem at hand. You see, change in and of itself is not hard to deal with.

It's our readiness for it, or perhaps even more importantly our lack thereof, that truly makes the difference. Simply put, <u>change is only hard for the unprepared</u>.

For example, imagine that you've been relocated for work and you have serious anxiety and stress about your new hometown. What will you do there? How will you make new friends? What if it isn't what you thought it would be? Before going to the "dark side" and deeming it a bad place to live, do your <u>research</u>.

What does the city have to offer that falls within your personal interests? Are there social groups or networking events you could get involved in to help you meet more people? What are others saying and what serves as a draw for those in the local community? Once you take a closer look, you might find your new home has more potential than you originally thought.

You may find you are now more receptive because you took the time to prepare yourself for what you could expect once you are there. The change is no longer thought of as something as tough to deal with as you thought. You've prepared yourself and now have a better idea of what to expect, which is how we really should handle life's major changes.

It's important to acknowledge that change comes in a variety of shapes and sizes, and some forms will certainly be easier to deal with than others. But resisting or deflecting the inevitable is nothing more than a drain on our time and talents. When we've taken on this mindset and change does come our way, it's no wonder we feel defensive.

If we aren't ready for it, how can we have the knowledge needed to move forward and continue? This lack of readiness is what causes us to suffer the most during times of change.

Preparing ourselves for what's next is a much more productive use of energy that will help rather than hinder us in moments of uncertainty. So how can we achieve this?

My advice is to <u>remain open-minded in times of change</u>. Rather than viewing it as a loss, see it as an opportunity. Consider finding a reason for why the change could be happening and trust that it's for your own good.

Instead of living in fear, consider whether the changes will serve as a teachable moment and make you stronger in the end.

Life is full of challenges. So why do we insist on making it harder than it already is? Whether we believe something to be possible or impossible — either way we are right. Working on our beliefs, staying open to what could be and being open to change requires less energy and leads to better outcomes.

Dealing with change doesn't have to be a struggle. It's only as tough as we make it. Let's be kinder to ourselves and vow to be ready and willing to handle whatever the future has to offer for a happier, more productive life.

Chapter Two

The Areas of Personal Change

Change happens whether we want it to or not. Some people welcome change and find ways to turn the unexpected into an opportunity for growth. Others become frightened and simply react. How we handle the inevitable changes in life is key to living a life without fear.

The right attitude can mean the difference between allowing unexpected life changes to keep us from achieving our goals or dealing with the changes and growing because of them.

When we are confronted with unforeseen changes in our lives, our first response may be to either run away from them or fight against them. Run or fight is an inborn survival instinct that occurs when we feel threatened.

Fueled by adrenaline, the fight or fight response is exhausting and can leave us feeling overwhelmed.

There are however, steps we can take to gain control of our fears and concerns, embrace the challenge, and turn our perceived misfortune into an avenue for success.

GAINING CONTROL OVER CHANGE

Our first response to sudden change is often panic. Rapid breathing, sweaty palms, and eye twitching are all signs of extreme alarm. These responses keep us from dealing with change in a positive way. Deep breathing is one of the easiest and most useful techniques we can use to calm and center ourselves.

THE THREE, SIX, NINE RULE

Exhale completely through your mouth, making a whoosh sound.

1. Close your mouth and inhale quietly through your nose to a count of three.

2. Hold your breath for a count of six.

• Exhale completely through your mouth, making a whoosh sound to a count of nine.

This is one breath. Now inhale again and repeat the cycle three more times for a total of four breaths.

Note, you always inhale quietly through your nose and exhale audibly through your mouth.

Exhaling takes three times as long as inhaling. The ratio of 3:6:9 is important.

Once you develop this technique by practicing it daily, it will be a useful tool that you will always have with you. Use it whenever anything upsetting happens — before you react. Use it whenever you feel internal tension or stress. Use it to help fall asleep.

Physical exertion is another great way to calm down and regain control. Take a walk or weed the garden. Being outdoors, in nature, is helpful, but the treadmill or exercise bike will work, too. Remember to take deep breaths; refrain from shallow breathing while exercising.

Clear your mind and do some deep breathing before retiring at night. Get up at the same time each morning. Don't use sleep to avoid dealing with the challenges you must face. Other useful techniques to calm stress include meditation, a warm bath, and aroma-therapy.

Once the panic response is under control, you can face the problem and think about solutions.

MEETING THE CHALLENGE

Give yourself time to adjust. Your mind and body will show you the way to meet the challenge if you just listen. Your attitude is crucial when dealing with adversity.

Train your mind to see the change to make something positive happen. Do not entertain negative thoughts.

Ask for direction from your spiritual force. We are all part of a universe that is much bigger than we are. Whether you call the source God, the universe, GUS (Guy Upstairs), nature, or your inner self, you are connected to a spiritual source. That source can not only help you through life's changes, but can point the way to success. Write down choices that you have in response to your change.

Ask yourself what are the consequences of each response to yourself, your friends, and your family? Picture yourself in the best-case scenario after you have succeeded at meeting this challenge. Believe it can happen. Believe in yourself.

HELPING YOU BECOME SUCCESSFUL AT CHANGE

Unexpected changes often take us by surprise. We may feel as if we have lost our footing and are swimming against a rip tide. But change can give birth to our greatest life successes if we open ourselves up to the possibilities.

Keep your values and remain true to yourself. Never compromise your beliefs even if it is expected or seems like it's the only way out at the time.

Think outside of yourself. How will your choices affect your friends, family, community, and the earth on which we live? You are part of a much larger world and if you make decisions that benefit others, you will benefit yourself.

Be patient. Turning change into success may not happen overnight.

Help others. While we may be going through change and adversity ourselves, it is through helping others that we truly grow and succeed.

Success is measured in different ways in our society. Most commonly, it is measured by how many cars or homes we own and how our possessions compare to our neighbors'.

The fact is that having money does not necessarily equal happiness. True happiness comes from meeting life's changes and overcoming challenges while remaining true to ourselves.

It's okay to be emotional. When faced with an unexpected change it is understandable to be emotional. Confusion, anger, fear, and sadness may be felt. We grieve the loss of what was perceived as normal and safe. Cry, scream, curl up on the couch, and reflect. But, do this for a <u>short</u> while only. These behaviors will not bring the past back, will not change the future, and will not make you feel better.

It's okay to give yourself permission to be vulnerable. When an unexpected change happens to you, the security of your world shifts and you may feel weak and uncertain of the future. Understand that facing this transition, we may be scared, vulnerable, weak, or in need of help from others. Allow yourself to rely on others. It may feel like you are exposed, but being completely exposed is not always a bad thing. There is always learning and growth that can come from it. Allowing people to really see that side of you, they can feel your stress or pain, and they can help.

It's okay to ask for help. When seeing someone else suffering, many people don't know what to say or what to do. After I went on medical leave from work there were people that didn't call me for several months, and these were people close to me. Some people get busy with their own daily life or they don't know what to say or what to do. There are others who are natural caregivers and jump right in to help . . . most people fall somewhere in the middle. It is your job to tell people what to say and what to do that will be helpful for you.

People are quick to say, "If you need anything just ask me," but deep inside they have no clue what you need. Sometimes when we go through major changes we think no one else can possibly understand or know what you are going through.

But there are others who can empathize with you. You're not alone.

Even if you don't ask people to be around you, family and close friends will come to your side. When asking for help, be specific. For me, going to the store was limited for six weeks. To ask someone to pick up my groceries for the week took a lot of pressure off my wondering how to get it accomplished. Asking a neighbor if she would get my prescription when she went to the drugstore solved a real problem for me and she was glad to help.

What I've learned is that I've had to ask very specifically for what I needed. Telling people how they can help you in very specific terms and what you need gives them a sense of purpose.

Left on their own to guess what you need they feel helpless as well, and when feeling helpless they may not offer to help.

If you need to talk, don't be afraid to ask someone to listen. Ask someone who has the time and compassion to hear how you feel. Talk out options, how the change has affected you, and what part of the past you are grieving about.

It's okay to have hope for the future. My health will never be back to what it was years ago, but I must continue to hope it will improve. Despite my setbacks, I have to believe that there is hope in my future. A belief I will get my blood sugar levels under control and the numbness in my feet and legs will allow me to continue my walks. Having that hope and having the positive perspective is what keeps me moving forward every day. If I gave up that belief it would be like letting my diabetes win. It would be telling me that all the efforts I am making now are for nothing.

I do not believe this. Believing that things can and will be different, helps me get through a change process.

It's okay to keep some of the old you. Going through a change, especially one that is traumatic, changes you forever. You will heal as a person, but you will never be the same. Changes often affect how you see life and deal with things. You're never going to be the same again and that's all right. Because during a change there is a great deal of learning . . . but only if you are willing to have vision and perspective.

Ask yourself "What am I supposed to be learning from this and how am I supposed to grow?" In any change process, you can become stronger, and a better version of you. Just because something changes around you, even something radical, doesn't change the core of who you are as a person. Sometimes you have to remind yourself of that.

Experiencing change can have a dramatic effect on our bodies as well as our minds. Millions of Americans watched the twin towers crumble and through the media were witness to the Atlanta shootings. Although a different experience to witness on a television, these unexpected events still can affect us emotionally, resulting in feelings of panic, fear, and vulnerability.

When you perceive an unexpected or sudden change, the body activates the stress response. The stress response occurs in both our body and brain leaving us feeling unsafe.

These responses can disrupt our beliefs and expectations about the world. Your feeling of being able to control your life may be shattered as you question how much influence you have over your life.

The body, mind, and soul all grieve the change including the loss of what was, and the anxiety of what will happen now.

THE PHYSICAL REACTIONS TO CHANGE

The body's response to acute stress is to begin to prepare for an emergency. Adrenaline and other hormones are released. The body shuts down processes associated with long-term care such as digestion, reproduction, and cell repair.

Survival is importance and there is an increase in blood sugar levels to provide energy for muscles. Blood pressure increases as blood is diverted from our extremities to our major muscles to provide us with extra strength. Increased endorphins are activated to help us ignore physical pain.

Changes to the body as a result of this perceived emergency can include a racing heart, dizziness, nausea, shortness of breath, shaking, feeling hot and flushed, and sweating. There can even be biological changes in the brain following the stress of a real or perceived sudden event or change.

Some ways to help prevent or reduce the physical symptoms may include eating sensible food, avoiding smoking or drinking alcohol, getting rest throughout the day, and exercise when possible.

THE EMOTIONAL REACTIONS TO CHANGE

Following a change, our beliefs and assumptions that we use to make sense of the world around us can change substantially. It's common to experience a wide range of psychological symptoms, including intrusive thoughts, worry, difficulty sleeping, trouble focusing, bouts of crying, blame or self-judgment, and lack of satisfaction.

The effects of sudden change can cause intense emotion including extreme emotional fluctuations, unhappiness, anxiety, loneliness, and anger.

Being around family or special friends who comfort you with soft words and hugs can be beneficial. This allows the emotional scars to be nurtured. Listening to music, looking at photos, or doing something nice for yourself can all contribute to your healing.

THE COGNITIVE REACTIONS TO CHANGE

Your mind has either accepted or not accepted the new change. With exposure to change resulting from trauma, parts of the brain associated with memory shrink, making it difficult to consolidate and form new memories. Repetitive stress affects our moods, brings on anxiety disorders, and affects our experience of chronic pain and ability to control food intake.

Short term memory problems and difficulty making decisions are two very common cognitive concerns following a sudden change or event. Your mind is in a temporary state of confusion and disorganization and needs time to catch up with the reality of the situation.

When one's stress is high, crying even discharges accumulating stress toxins that are in our tears. Unfortunately, in our current society, refusing to cry, suffering in silence, and "being strong" are often viewed as admirable and desirable reactions. Crying, on the other hand is seen as a weakness.

THE SPIRITUAL REACTIONS TO CHANGE

Sudden change can shake one's religious faith or lead to its rebirth. As healing progresses, people might discover the potential for greater religious faith, perhaps becoming more receptive to spiritual development after such an experience.

Scientific polling among Americans reveals ninety percent of Americans believe in God. However, it has been shown that a commitment rather than simply believing is more important in predicting health outcomes. Religious commitment means putting belief into practice, or action. It measures the depth of one's faith.

This includes a relationship with God, making beliefs an important part of one's life, and connecting with others in the religious community.

People who are religiously committed are often more satisfied with life and more adaptable to change. They are often mentally and physically healthier, live longer, and are less stressed.

Self-esteem is fostered by knowing that one matters and that they are loved. As one religious man said, *"I take comfort in knowing that I am a child of a loving God, with worth and potential."*

Sometimes under the stress of living and the many changes we experience, it is easy for us to lose sight of the meaning and purpose of life. Faith is what sees us through the bumps in the road and helps us reclaim life's balance.

> "If there is a meaning in life at all, then there must be a meaning in suffering and in dying." —Viktor Frankl

Religious communities can support and guide us in difficult situations when we stumble.

There is a comfort in knowing someone is looking down on me lovingly and generously and compassionately — someone who is trying to help me out. I grow stronger thinking God and my father and others who have gone before me are watching and guiding me.

For many, an unexpected change such as a diagnosis of terminal illness brings on "death anxiety." Religion and one's faith can help face death with greater peace.

In my years as a Hospice counselor, I saw many people who fought death. They were denying that it was happening and always looking for a cure. The shock of learning you have a life-threatening illness can cause one to feel life is over already. Dreading death in this manner takes away the joy of living.

We can learn to accept death but enjoy the precious moments of life as well. In fact, death denial takes energy. Releasing this energy allows us to focus more fully on life. If you fear for the loved ones who survive you, prepare them as best as you can, which is all you can do.

Your loved ones will grieve—if you let them know that grieving is permissible. They will eventually mourn and move beyond their grief.

Some people find a belief in the afterlife a comfort in the death of loved ones.

One night following my son's death, I dreamed that he appeared and told me he was all right. He told me to keep doing what I was doing to help others over the trauma of losing a child. I took great comfort in this dream, which affirmed my belief in an afterlife and that my loved ones will be waiting.

Many people, including myself, struggle to surrender control. Religion teaches us to share control and to accept the loss of control with greater peace. Trusting that God will ensure that all things work out, helps us to accept those things.

It is my purpose to share education, personal beliefs, and information in this chapter. I do not intend to persuade, agree, or disagree with any other belief system you may have.

LIFE REVIEW
Many of the perceptions people have about change were developed when they were children. Without new information or added options introduced to them, they continue to believe this is the only way to behave.

Telling a child to stop crying and be strong following a decision to move from their home may hinder their emotional development throughout the rest of their life. They may have left a best friend in the previous location, and now are reluctant to develop attachments.

Believing that displays of affection show weakness, they may hold things inside rather than deal openly with them.

Businesses often give their workers little notice regarding a transfer, downsize, or dismissal.

Little regard is often given to the workers and their new changes and expectations. Gone is the security of the job, the co-workers, and the income.

Completing a change history reveals how a person and their family dealt with those changes in the past. The information can be an indicator as to how you will deal with a current or future change. Understanding when dealing with a change, you will discover what is normal for you. This information can be invaluable to your recovery as you work through your grief.

CHANGES IN YOUR LIFE

Changes in our lives are not limited to locations. Have you experienced change with friends, pets, a home, or a job? Did you spend years changing schools, moving to new areas, or getting different jobs? These can all involve emotional changes.

Therefore, your change history should not only be births and deaths, but divorces, job changes, both mental and physical illnesses, and major moves or any other changes significant to you.

- Did you have a longtime friend who moved away? Did you go away to college or take a job in a new city? These transitions can be seen as changes and should be included.

- With each change you write down, think back to your reactions, emotions, and feelings at the time. Jot down a few words that come to mind that remind you of how you felt.

- Who was there to talk to you about these changes? How did members of your family deal with your feelings and their own feelings?

- Did the others around you understand your needs and give you time to adjust?

Chapter Three

Understanding Emotions and Feelings

Every change has an emotional effect on the person experiencing that change. Every change in our lives affects us and costs us something.

Realizing, recognizing, and acknowledging the emotions of change can help you better deal with your change and help others through their changes. Accepting someone else's emotions goes a long way towards helping them deal with their situation. Change can be hard either way, but if you ignore the emotions you'll find yourself always battling to make change successful.

Change often brings on **fear** because it can be scary when it takes you into something unknown and potentially serious. With any change, there can be a **sense of loss.** Grieving for what was and missing the comfort that was left behind is natural.

Having to give up working when my health declined caused me to fear the future. How would I pay my bills? Would I ever return to work? I grieved the pleasure I received from working.

We may feel an emptiness because of our loss. People may have loved the way things were. Knowing the change was needed people still may grieve what they left behind. People often get mad about a change. **Anger** "boils up to the surface" and people say and do things they may later regret. We may say or do things that are mostly out of character for us. Change often takes something away from people, especially in the beginning.

Feelings of **confusion** may develop when facing a change. These feelings may last until we can process the news, adjust to the change, and understand what the new reality will be like. When the change is not only not expected, but sudden it can leave a person feeling numb. Often in such an emotional "shock" we do not know what to feel or how to responds to the news.

> Losing my son, for me, was like losing a limb. Part of my existence was now gone. The part of me known as Jeremy's mom had vanished.

For some people, change can bring on a feeling of **enthusiasm.** This is a good and positive emotion, except for the people around them who are having difficulty with the change. The members of the group's enthusiasm can further irritate another person's pain.

People who have experienced very painful emotions following a change, have often learned to control their pain by shutting down their emotions. It is as if they think, "Feelings are too painful—I refuse to feel."

They might have picked up messages along the way that reinforce this decision not to feel.

- If showing emotions or feeling such as crying, showing tenderness, or displaying anger were mocked, it may be because we were conditioned to stuff emotions inside. They may have grown up in a stoic dynamic where feelings simply were not expressed. In families who were too preoccupied with survival to feel, there may have been little time or luxury to share feelings.

- Spoken or unspoken messages might inaccurately emphasize that soldiers, policemen, firefighters, doctors, or nurses shouldn't cry. That in doing so they would be perceived as sissies, weaklings, and unable to perform.

- Self-talk fear messages, such as "I won't be respected if I show my feelings" or "If I feel at all, I will lose control and not be able to regain it" can cause some to refrain from showing feelings.

IMPORTANCE OF EMOTIONS

Feelings make us human and yet can serve as protective shields. Even with a protective shield, some people lose control of their emotions in unwholesome ways. They say things in the heat of emotion that they later regret, or lacking proper coping skills, use violence and uncontrolled anger in inappropriate ways. This behavior might also be the case with those who repeatedly give in to their fears.

The wholesome release of emotions returns our system to equilibrium, to be prepared to react to the next emergency. Those who remain on constant alert are often the ones who blow up or burn out.

Some people seem to feel little, but often they do feel, their intense emotions have just been numbed. Those emotions remain just under the surface, ready to explode. Often, anger is the closest emotion to the surface and covers up emotions such as fear and hurt. If only the anger is experienced and expressed, the other emotions will never begin to heal. Our goal then, is to be fully aware of the full range of feelings, and their stages so that we can channel them constructively.

> We need to feel and experience fear. Without fear, we don't take wise precautions. Without anger, some protective acts would not be introduced. If we pay attention to it, grief tells us where healing is needed. Uncomfortable feelings tell us that something is wrong so that we can take appropriate action.

Numb feelings initially protect us from our overwhelming emotions, then send a sign for healing later. Without fully feeling, we do not fully respond to life. To shut down some of our feelings is to shut all the positive ones down too.

Our goal, then, is to learn to experience and express feelings as normal, constructive, and wholesome. If we don't, we are more likely to experience intrusions, rage, bodily complaints, fatigue, and self-destruction.

Anxiety is worrisome thoughts plus excessive emotional and physical reactions. When the brain perceives a threat, it sets off a chain of physical changes that prepares the body for fight or flight. This is the beginning of stress.

Messages are sent through nerves and blood-borne hormones to the body's various organs. Muscles tense, the heart beats faster and stronger, and the rate of breathing increases. The brain becomes sharper and able to react more quickly.

Stress is very adaptive and prepares the body for emergencies. The energy of the stress response is designed to be worked off physically and the body then returns to the resting state.

In anxiety, the mind stays alert which keeps the emotions and the body stirred. The nervous system becomes over-stimulated and the brain's alarm centers sound the alarm for even smaller threats. Being in this state causes the body to take longer to return to a calm and relaxed state.

When this happens, anxiety seems to take on a life of its own. The subsequent feelings are not always appropriate to what is going on in your life.

Symptoms of anxiety can be felt in four areas of the body in different ways: physical, emotional, mental, and spiritual.

Physical fatigue includes feelings of tension, fatigue, trembling, tingling, nausea, digestive tract problems, rapid breathing, pounding heart, feelings of suffocating, and panic attacks.

Emotional fatigue is characterized by irritation, moodiness, exaggerated emotions such as fear, and loss of confidence.

Mental fatigue includes confusion and an inability to concentrate, remember, or make appropriate decisions. The mind is not able to focus properly.

Spiritual fatigue exhibits feelings of misery, hopelessness, and depression.

Remember, the symptoms of anxiety are merely an exaggerated stress response. They lessen as we retrain our nervous system to be calmer. They increase as we tell ourselves that things are unbearable and must stop.

> Being anxious about change is common in most humans, but through education and training it can be controlled.

Chapter Four

Taking Care of Your Health

Nutrition is one of the first things neglected when someone is stressed or anxious about a change. The mind and body work together. The condition of your body will profoundly affect your mood, energy level, and performance. Developing a healthier body will help you become more resilient to unexpected changes. Physical wellness is about taking care of your body for optimal health and functioning.

I am an emotional eater. If I am sad I eat junk food, if I am happy I celebrate with food. Any change in my life gave me the incentive to eat. Who ever felt depressed and said, "I think I will eat a bowl of broccoli"? It is the sugar, the comfort those foods bring us. I ate myself right into type 2 diabetes and now changing my diet is no longer by choice, it is a necessity.

In an effort to remain in control of your emotions while going through a change, try to include a "rainbow" of fruits and vegetables at every meal or snack. Eat an array of foods from various sources to ensure a balanced intake of nutrients.

Start the day with a nutritious breakfast. Rather than rush through your meals, try to relax and enjoy them. Eat slowly and mindfully.

Stock your home and car with healthy snacks: yogurt, fruit, energy bars, trail mix, or cheese. You will be less tempted to reach for high calorie choices if healthy ones are readily available.

One of my biggest downfalls with emotional eating is I never crave healthy foods. I drive through a fast food or order a pizza to pick up on my way home. Having something in the car or office that is salty and sweet but is healthy reduces my poor eating choices.

Stay hydrated to feel good and perform well. There are times I have reached for food, only to find I was really just thirsty.

When beginning my new food plan, I was told to drink one ounce of water daily for every two pounds of my weight. At my weight at the time, I thought this was crazy. But in doing so, I found I craved less soda, have less of a desire to snack, and began to feel better.

Learn to respond to signals of hunger and fullness. They are your portion control guides. Eat 3 meals and between meal snacks to keep yourself energized and to avoid extremes of hunger.

BODY MOVEMENT
There are several health benefits to getting your body moving! Exercising helps reduce feelings of anxiety and depression, helps prevent and manage stress, and promotes mental well-being. Being active helps us maintain

healthy bones, muscles, and joints. It decreases the risk of heart disease, stroke, diabetes, and high blood pressure.

Adults should try to be physically active for at least 30 minutes for 5 days per week. If your change concerns your health, you may feel you need to start exercising right away after years of living a sedentary life. Start slowly. No pain, no gain is a myth! Do activities that you enjoy such as dancing, bowling, basketball, yoga, walking, or biking.

The key is to develop a healthy lifestyle of activities and habits. You do not need to begin with a 5 mile walk or swimming 100 laps. Start small and break it up into small segments.

To help control my diabetes and develop better habits following the increase in my blood sugar, I joined the YMCA and began taking a beginner's class. When I need to stop, I stop and when I need to rest, I rest. The instructor starts each class by saying "If it hurts, stop." Motivation will suffer if we are in pain the next day.

When my doctor told me, walking would help my diabetes and circulation, I was embarrassed and discouraged that I could only walk one-fourth of a mile. In time, I have increased to one mile. When I get discouraged at my slow progress, I remind myself that this is a 400% improvement. A lifetime of being a couch-potato will not change overnight. But looking at the positive side of this new change helps me continue to try to accomplish it every day.

EXERCISE

Almost everyone I spoke to who engages in a regular, moderate exercise program says how effective it is in reducing their stress. Exercise has been shown to reduce muscle tension and other stress symptoms without the side effects of medication. Improved self-esteem and mental health are felt. There is reduced blood pressure, increased energy levels, and a decline in heart and breathing rates. Exercise can improve the quality of your sleep, promote weight loss, and strengthen the immune system.

When the body is engaged in physical movement, the stress response is conditioned to decline. Exercise allows the body to expend the energy of the stress response and return it to a more restful state. It also gives the mind a break and time to disengage and flow free, so following exercise we are both mentally and physically refreshed.

Some people think they are too busy to exercise. It helps me to think of exercise as an important investment in my mind and body. Exercise enables people to be more productive and accomplish more things in less time. It also enables them to remain more relaxed and in a better frame of mind while they cope with the changes.

Daily, gentle exercise is best for stress reduction and weight loss. It has been reported that even a ten minute energy walk can bring ninety minutes of energy, elevated mood, and stress reduction.

Start your exercise program gently and build up gradually. You are not in a race. Exercise should leave you refreshed and energized. Any exercise is a benefit to your body. Exercising can also help you enjoy a restful sleep.

If you are older or have any health risk factors such as being overweight or diabetes, family history of high blood pressure or heart disease have a physical examination beforehand and discuss your exercise plans with your doctor.

Speaking of sleep, poor sleep can be both a cause and effect of anxiety and change. Sleep researchers believe that almost all adults function and feel at their best with at least eight hours of sleep. Some people however, do better on more, and some are productive with considerably less sleep.

Getting consistent and adequate sleep helps your body and mind rest and repair. It protects you from illness and helps regulate weight. Sleep helps us maintain good mental health.

Consistent sleep and wake-up times are needed to keep the body's sleep cycle regular. Retiring at irregular hours such as getting to bed much later Friday and Saturday nights than on weekdays can lead to insomnia. People often complain about the difficulty in getting up and going on Mondays.

Several inventions have interfered with sleep. The Internet and worldwide communication allows people to work or be entertained around the clock. The invention of the light bulb permits people to stay up later and do shift work. Television programs including a twenty-four-hour shopping channel promotes irregular sleep patterns. It is no wonder that today's American is sleep-deprived.

Unexpected change can disrupt sleep.

TIPS TO GETTING A BETTER SLEEP

Naps are okay if they are not your primary way of getting sleep. Limit the length of your naps so they don't interfere with your ability to sleep at night. Remove phones, computers, and television from the bedroom. Don't pay bills, work, or read arousing material in bed. If you are having difficulty sleeping, either eliminate naps altogether, or try them regularly each day for fifteen to ninety minutes around 1:00–2:00 P.M.

Reduce light and noise. They can disturb sleep. If your clock emits light, cover it or turn it away from you.

Don't eat a big meal within four hours of retiring. If you must eat, a light snack such as warm milk, crackers and cheese, or sweetened yogurt can help you fall asleep quicker.

Avoid stimulants like caffeine for at least seven to ten hours before bedtime.

Once in bed, try slow breathing or progressive muscle relaxation to unwind.

Chapter Five

Self-Care Suggestions

Many people are surprised to learn that very subtle shifts in breathing can cause anxiety symptoms ranging from muscle tension to migraines, panic attacks, and high blood pressure.

Breathing affects the way we think and feel, the quality of what we create, and how we function in our daily life. Normal breathing is slow, effortless, regular, and quiet with practically no movement above the diaphragm.

When experiencing unexpected changes, our heart rates and breathing escalates. For optimal breathing, the goals are to change from erratic quick breathing to slow, regular, rhythmic abdominal breathing and to make this kind of breathing automatic.

Begin practicing this breathing when you are home or in a safe environment.

- **Loosen your clothing.** Lie on your back or in the half-lying position. Place pillows under your back and knees to relax the abdominal muscles.
- **Relax** your entire body.
- **Breathe** comfortably through your nose to the count of six or seven. As you breathe in, let your stomach rise slowly. Hold the breath for six or seven seconds and slowly exhale to the count of six or seven.

Practice twice a day or more, for five to ten minutes each time. For the first few days, just breathe at your regular rate.

You may experience some dizziness and faintness from improper breathing. These symptoms usually disappear if you get up and walk around a bit. When you resume practice, *be sure that you are not breathing fast or deeply, only slowly and regularly.*

Remember, first relax your entire body, then breathe slowly, regularly. As you gain confidence, in preparation for future changes in your life, try consciously re-breathing in slightly stressful situations such as in a traffic slow-down before anxiety symptoms appear.

Finally, when you feel ready, try doing it in situations where anxiety symptoms have already begun to appear. Notice the symptoms. Think to yourself, "My breathing is causing this. I'm not going mad or having a heart attack. I know how to breathe." Then relax your body, and breathe slowly and regularly.

OTHER SUGGESTIONS

Visualizing air being drawn through the toes into the abdomen and pelvis helps to slow down breathing. As you practice, think, "Low and slow."

Some people find it helpful to visualize being on the beach, breathing in refreshing air and likening the breath to the easy rhythm of the waves.

Practice 333 breathing. Breathe in to the count of three. Hold the normal breath for a count of three, then breathe out slowly, hold to three, then resume easy abdominal breathing.

Relaxation is the opposite of stress. In stress, both the mind and body are stimulated. Muscle tension in the anxious body keeps the nervous system alerted.

Relaxation means that the mind and body are calm. As the mind and body remain in a calm state of reduced stimulation, they become restored. This allows the nervous system to desensitize.

Because the mind and body are connected, relaxation can be achieved when the body is relaxed, and the mind follows, or by relaxing the mind and letting the body follow.

Relaxation is a skill that improves with practice. Most methods recommend practicing once or twice each day, working yourself up to twenty minutes each time. If possible, find a quiet place free from interruptions. Relaxation techniques usually ask that you focus on one thing rather than scattering your attention. A singular focus allows the mind to calm down.

Some people write down their worries and then put them in an imaginary box before relaxing. Others simply say, "I'll deal with you later, but right now I am going to relax."

Relaxation training works best after exercise or yoga, when the body is calming down and the mind is clear. Relaxation after eating may seem like a good idea, but digestion seems to interfere with relaxation, so it is best not to practice right after a meal.

Remember, learning to relax is the process . . . something most people are not use to. Don't expect an immediate outcome.

Rise slowly after relaxation training. Allow ample time for your blood pressure to return to normal. Some people feel as if they are floating or losing track of time as they relax.

Change affects all the parts of our mind and body. You might be surprised to find that your anxiety occasionally seems to increase as you try to relax.

This is normal. As we relax, we are usually more aware of our physical symptoms, such as tension. We also may be more aware of our troublesome thoughts. Some people feel like they are vulnerable and out of control when relaxing.

For example, if one had been abused while lying down, then lying down now might understandably feel frightening. If we are carrying around suppressed fears or worries, relaxing will let down our guard, allowing those fears come into our awareness. This is like the person who suppresses worries all day by keeping busy but then becomes preoccupied with the worries at night when he wants to sleep. Others might worry that they should be accomplishing something tangible rather than relaxing.

Originally developed in Europe, another effective relaxation method is simply to **give yourself the suggestions of warmth and heaviness** to induce deep relaxation.

1. Start by sitting or lying comfortably, with eyes closed if that is comfortable, breathing abdominally.

2. Imagine that you have just returned from a refreshing walk and you are sinking into an overstuffed chair. Let the abdomen and chest be warm and soft. You slowly repeat to yourself each of these suggestions three times: "My right arm is heavy." "My right hand is heavy." "My fingers are heavy."

This is repeated for the left arm and hand, the right leg and foot, and then the left leg and foot.

3. Following this step begin saying to yourself "My right arm is warm," and so on. Upon completion of this sequence, you end the exercise by imagining that you are relaxing in a warm tub of water, or lying on a blanket on the beach with a relaxed smile on your face.

MEDITATION

When in meditation, we go beneath our worries and racing thoughts, and begin to rest in the center of our being, which is a calm and peaceful place.

In meditation, we simply allow our mind to release and relax. Think of your mind as a pool of water. When agitated, it swirls, but when relaxed the water can settle and become clear. Your mind will become clearer as it settles beneath your racing thoughts and fears.

Meditation involves letting go of the tension of your body to bring a sense of relaxation. It is performed by constricting and releasing your various muscle groups. The idea is that by relieving the stress you have built up throughout your body, you can quiet and calm your mind.

Before you begin relaxation or meditation get into a comfortable position in a place that is free of distraction. You can start off sitting in a chair or lying down. Close your eyes if that feels best for you and then work your way through the following steps:

1. Breathe. Begin with a <u>deep breathing exercise</u>. Inhale deeply through your nose, feeling your abdomen rise as you fill your body with air. Then slowly exhale out

the mouth, the navel pulling in toward the spine as you expel the stale air out. Repeat 3-5 cycles of deep breathing.

2. Tighten and release your muscles. Start with your feet by clenching your toes and pressing your heels toward the ground. Squeeze tightly for a few breaths and then release. Now flex your feet in, pointing your toes up towards your head. Hold for a few seconds and then release.

3. Continue to work your way up your body, tightening and then letting go of each muscle group. Work your way up to your legs, abdomen, back, hands, arms, shoulders, neck, and face.

4. Try to tighten each muscle group for a few breaths and then slowly release. You can repeat any areas that feel especially stiff.

5. Notice any differences you feel between tightening your muscles and relaxing them.

6. End your practice by taking a few more deep breaths, noting how much more calm and relaxed you feel.

Just like learning any new skill, relaxation requires practice. By practicing several times a week, you will become more aware of what it's like to feel relaxed. Understanding this feeling can help you to more readily let go of tension when anxiety rises. Being able to quickly relax your body can also help you in <u>managing stress</u> and panic attacks.

Practice meditation once or twice daily for at least a week. Do so for about five minutes each time, increasing gradually to about twenty minutes.

Guided Imagery is a form of meditation. It can help you emotionally and physically. Many times stress from the events prior, during, and after an unexpected change cause physical strains. Finding a calm place within yourself can be beneficial when your emotions get too difficult to face.

Any place that brings a smile to your heart.

Let's take a mini trip to the beach. Get yourself in a comfortable position. Close your eyes if you are comfortable doing so. Take a deep breath to the count of three through your nose. Hold it for three seconds and exhale for six seconds. Repeat this once more. Visualize yourself at the beach. It could be morning as the sun is rising or later in the day when the sun is setting or even late at night. As you look around, what do you see? Are there other people or are you alone? If there are people, are they fishing, walking, or like you, just enjoying the day? Walk a bit down the beach, put your hand down and pick up some sand. Run it through your fingers. Is the sand dry and fine like the sand when you first enter the beach? Is the sand wet like the sand at the water's edge or soft like the sand warmed by the sun?

If you are wearing shoes and socks, sit down and remove them. Take a few steps and put your toes in the water. Is the water warm like bath water or chilly like early summer in the north? What do you hear? Can you hear waves? Birds? People talking? Someone playing a radio? Thunder as a storm approaches? Lastly, what can you smell—the salt in the air? The fish someone may have caught? The smell of food grilling? The time has come to go home. Pick up your shoes and start walking back to the road.

Take a deep breath to the count of three through your nose. Hold it for three seconds and exhale for six seconds. Repeat this once more.

Guided imagery is one of the relaxation techniques I taught to the staff at the Hospice I worked for. It gave them a calming way to end the day after emotional and difficult cases.

Chapter Six

Being Happy, Resilient, and Balanced

Without a doubt, technological advances such as laptops and smart phones have created the best of times and the worst of times. It's hardly a surprise that the word "burn-out" came into use as our technology increased. It can feel like we're at the mercy of technology and that coping with all the changes in our lives is our full-time job.

While we may not like the change that is happening, we cannot keep it from happening, but we can control how we react. Whining and complaining about our fate and assuming the victim posture will not benefit us. Acknowledging our discomfort and saying to ourselves, "This has happened and it's not fair, but what can I do about it?"

We can invest our energy in feeling sorry for ourselves or we can invest it in figuring out how to adapt and thrive.

Change is inevitable. But whether it seems positive or negative or is planned or unplanned, it can be difficult to cope with. Change is hard. It puts us in unfamiliar situations, and unfamiliar situations can feel uncomfortable even when they are positive.

Expecting change to feel hard helps us because it eases our discomfort. It permits us to assign responsibility for our discomfort to the right cause.

Then when the going gets tough, we aren't surprised. We can say to ourselves, "This is exactly what I was expecting. This is normal. I will feel better when this new situation begins to feel more familiar. It's just a matter of time."

If the change is planned, prepare for it by thinking about what you can do to make it feel easier, and deciding what to do if it gets too hard.

If you find it hard to adjust to moving to a new home, set up your new bedroom right away. This way at least one room feels organized and familiar. Or stay with family for a few days until your new home feels more organized. Invite friends over as soon as possible so that the new place starts to feel like your home. Keeping what is familiar during change—sticking to a familiar routine, doing familiar work, seeing familiar people, going to familiar places—helps tremendously

Because it is familiar, we tend to hold on to the past. Think of the music you listen to or the movies you stop at when flipping through the channels. Familiar feels safe. If we keep running back to the safety of the past, we cannot move forward. The sooner we accept that change is happening, the sooner we can feel better about it.

Gently accepting the fact that change is happening is helpful. Demanding that we accept it is not. Gently accepting change means facing our fears, dealing with them appropriately, and taking the time we need to deal with them.

The sooner we get to a place of acceptance, the sooner we can take the next steps. The sooner we can move forward—the sooner we can start to make our todays beautiful. When we're going through change, as much as we try to do well in other areas of our life, sometimes we simply cannot. Beating ourselves up about it only makes us feel worse. Recognizing that change is hard and making allowances for time to accept it helps. By being gentle with ourselves and giving ourselves a free pass occasionally we are better able to make the transition.

When changes are really hard to get through, the important thing is to get through them in the healthiest way possible. There is nothing wrong with asking for help. It is the responsible and mature thing to do. Suffering silently and alone when other options are available is painful and not effective.

The early stages of loss and change are similar and include shock and denial. People in this stage often refuse to believe what has happened and instead believe everything will be all right. They may have feelings of guilt at not having done or said more and being angry at the situation, someone else, or even at God for placing them in their situation. Once someone passes through the several stages to the one of acceptance, they can move on.

When the change results from organizational issues, there may also be additional "negotiations." In an effort to avoid the change, the affected person may offer to work harder or longer hours as a way of preventing or slowing down the change.

Everyone experiencing a change does not go through all the stages, and for those who do, it may not be a smooth process. The quicker you get to the "acceptance" stage, the better things will be.

Communications are always important, but especially when you face change. With a personal or organizational change, a lack of communications with others can have a negative impact.

You need details about the change so that you can determine how it will affect you. Don't just sit back and wait for things to happen. Talk to your boss and your co-workers to get their inputs and understanding.

Part of the fear of change involves dealing with the unknown. If possible, try to minimize this factor by talking to others who have undergone such a change. What difficulties did they experience and how did they deal with them?

Change requires flexibility. The better able you are to adapt to change, the greater your chances of being successful.

Look at the requirements of the new situation. Although your current job may not be exactly like the new one, what skills from your old position can you apply to the new situation? Consider how you can adapt your own skills in life to your new environment.

Keeping a positive attitude can help you deal with the uncertainties of change. For example, instead of worrying about changes you must make, focus instead on how you can leverage your existing skills and experience. Looking for opportunities in the new organization, and becoming involved will hasten your adjustment.

Remember this: *Familiar feels good because it feels normal. Change feels hard because it* does *not feel normal. If we keep trying to find the old normal in our new, changed situation, we will continue to struggle.*

The old normal no longer exists, but a new normal is possible. When we establish new patterns for ourselves, those new patterns start to feel familiar. They will become our new normal. And that new normal will begin to feel good too.

Ultimately, change is what we make of it. We can make it as good as it can be, or continue to hold onto the past. The choice is yours.

Self-esteem helps protect most people from anxiety and stress. Self-esteem is one of the most important predictors of a life filled with happiness and satisfaction. Investing time into building self-esteem is worthwhile and beneficial.

Self-esteem can be developed, regardless of one's history or circumstances. Self-esteem is an accurate, honest, and appreciative opinion of oneself. It is having positive feelings and liking oneself.

Having self-esteem is not having an unrealistically high opinion of one's self or one's abilities. Self-esteem is not the same as being selfish or self-centered. Self-esteem is not destructive pride or ego that says we are better than another person or that we are more capable or self-reliant than we truly are. This would be considered arrogance and deception.

People with self-esteem retain a healthy humility as they are aware of their strengths and weaknesses.

They admit they have weaknesses, but know these weaknesses are viewed only as "rough edges" and are not the totality of who they are. Deep down inside they are quietly glad to be who they are and this satisfaction motivates them to continue to grow and improve.

The person with self-esteem has the tools to adapt to unexpected changes.

As people recover and grow from change, the happiness that once appeared permanently taken away will begin to return. The capacity for pleasure and the ability to laugh begin to resurface.

Experiencing feelings of pleasure, happiness, and a sense of humor are signs that healing is taking place. These feelings also help us to enjoy life and protect us against distress. The happier people are, the less distressed they feel.

WHAT PREDICTS HAPPINESS FOR PEOPLE?

Many of the factors listed to predict happiness are the same factors that help treat or prevent negative reactions to unexpected change or trauma. Most are things we <u>can</u> do something about like having good self-esteem, peace of mind, and a religious commitment. These include healthy habits such as regular exercise, sufficient sleep, and smart eating.

Happy people are more involved with friends, family, organizations, and rewarding social interaction. They reach out and invest themselves to form supportive relationships with others and are more outgoing and sociable.

They have an active involvement in life. Happy people are more likely to submerge themselves in things they find meaningful or satisfying such as family, work, and pleasant activities. They don't sit around passively waiting for life to happen to them — they seek out the opportunity.

Happy people work at mastering positive coping styles and control. They are committed to problem solving and are not passive or helpless. They show initiative, have control over their time, and are organized. Rather than procrastinating, happy people spend their time planning, moving and progressing toward meaningful goals. Goals are somewhat modest, but they are realistic and achievable, thus providing more satisfaction.

Happy people anticipate pleasure and expect something good to happen and that things will go well. They reason that whatever happens, it will be for the best. Happy people can grow from change. They see the benefits and rewards of accepting their new normal.

There was a saying "fake it until you make it" that was used in substance abuse programs I worked in. "Acting" like a clean and sober person until you could be one increased the chances of success. Acting like a happy person, then, could increase happiness and thereby reduce anxiety, depression, and stress. And one day, you will discover you are a happy person.

Change is a permanent part of our lives. Many of the changes that happen in our lives, we are not prepared for or even know how to move on from in life after they happen. There is no magic wand that will make the changes in life stop coming, but you can learn to be more prepared.

Remember what helped me through my unexpected changes, my "bumps in the road."

Journaling! Take the thoughts that are in your mind and put them to words on paper.

Research! When faced with an unexpected change, go to the library, go on-line, take a class. Whatever will get you more informed to overcome and triumph over that change.

Talk to people! Don't sit alone worrying and fearing the change. Talk to friends, family, members of a support group with members who are facing the same change.

Create a plan! You know that you cannot make the change go away. Sit down and write out a plan. Decide what you need to do about this change to make your life better and more normal. Maybe there is something you can do about the change. Maybe the plan will involve changing the way you look and feel about the change.

Optimism is not the naive expectation that everything will turn out rosy. It is instead, an attitude that no matter what happens, you can find something to enjoy. It is your choice to be happy despite obstacles and change.

A Message from Mary Jane

When we encounter a speed bump in the road, we are usually given a sign, before the bump, to let us know to slow down and proceed with caution. That doesn't always happen in real life. In our lives, the bumps in the road are often a surprise and usually unexpected. Having been through my share of bumps, I now help others over the bumps in their own paths.

My life has been filled with bumps in the road that I was not prepared for. I was the 12th child born to my parents. Shortly before the birth of my twin brother and me, my father left the family and moved on to another woman with whom he had additional children.

My first bump in the road involved being placed with a new family. Although I was not aware of this when I was eight months old, I grew up knowing I was adopted and somewhat different than others. To not only accept change, but to grow from it is something I learned at an early age, and I now share this knowledge with others.

WHAT HAS HELPED ME OVER MY BUMPS IN THE ROAD?
This is how I personally used the tools I suggest for you at the end of the previous chapter.

Journaling! Taking the thoughts that are in my mind and putting them to words on paper helps my brain find solutions. Doing this helps me to sort my thoughts out and begin to make sense of my situation.

Research! When I was getting my divorce, I read the laws and learned how to protect my boys and myself, and how to go about getting the back child support that my children deserved. This taught me how to survive on my own and to not be so hurt that I closed my heart to others.

Talking to people! Find people that care and know what you are going through. There are always going to be gossips and nosy people. But the task is to find those people who care about lifting you up. People who have been through a similar bump and can offer advice, education, and empathy can help guide you over your bumps.

Create a plan! When I discovered I was going to become a single mom of four growing boys, someone who hadn't work much in years, I looked for a job. I worked from home to avoid babysitter costs. I considered government programs to help us out for a short time until I could stand alone. I enrolled in college to better myself.

My final piece of advice is to *just look towards the future*. Sitting and feeling sorry for the bump you were given will not help or make it disappear.

If you found this information helpful, I invite you to leave your review on Amazon.

CONNECT WITH MARY JANE ON SOCIAL MEDIA

CounselorMary   comfortingarm   http://bit.   http://bit.
                                     ly/2k4IY6D   ly/2mTOedQ

To sign up for Mary Jane Cronin's *Bumps in the Road Newsletter* register at: http://www.maryjanecronin.com/mary-jane-s-blog.html

Other Books by
Mary Jane Cronin

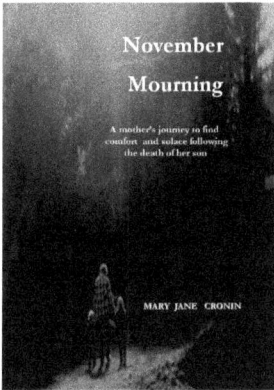

November Mourning

Mary Jane Cronin has written not just a fact-filled book about loss and grief, but one that included her personal journey to understand, accept and heal following the 1998 murder of her own son. *November Mourning* offers insight and hope as it explores the many emotions parents often feel following the loss of a child. Travel with Mary Jane through denial and anger as her own quest leads her to one day find acceptance and comfort. Learn about the stages of grief and techniques to help move through them easier. Discover what other parents have said and done to help reduce their own suffering. Recognize the physical and emotional symptoms of grief. See how people can help or hinder your healing. Research has shown it does not matter whether their child was a newborn or an adult, the natural order of life these parents have come to trust, and their very existence and purpose are forever changed. *November Mourning* addresses the many emotions parents may face in a world they now know holds no promises of safety or longevity.

ISBN: 978-0615239781

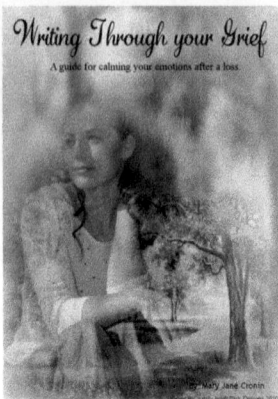

Writing Through Your Grief

This is a guidebook to help you through a loss. Losing someone you love is difficult. Trying to continue in a world without them is even more difficult. *Writing Through your Grief* offers you an opportunity to reflect on your time together, your emotions and the way you have dealt with grief in the past. Through the writing prompts, you will share stories, and learn about the healing process. Although you will never be "over" it, it is my hope you will one day be able to smile when you share stories about them . . . rather than fill with tears.

ISBN: 978-0984501601

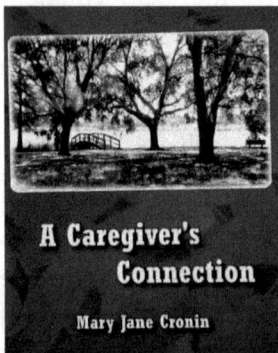

A Caregiver's Connection

People are living longer these days. The result is often "longer not better" with illness and limitations requiring a caregiver to step in and help with their care. The description of that caregiver is often a wife or daughter with a family of their own. Many sons and husbands are also taking on this role with little or no training and knowledge of what to do. Providing these services while working themselves, caregivers may neglect their own care. *A Caregiver's Connection* offers resources, writing prompts and self-care for the caregivers.

ISBN: 978-0984501625

All books available at:
http://www.maryjanecronin.com/book-store.html